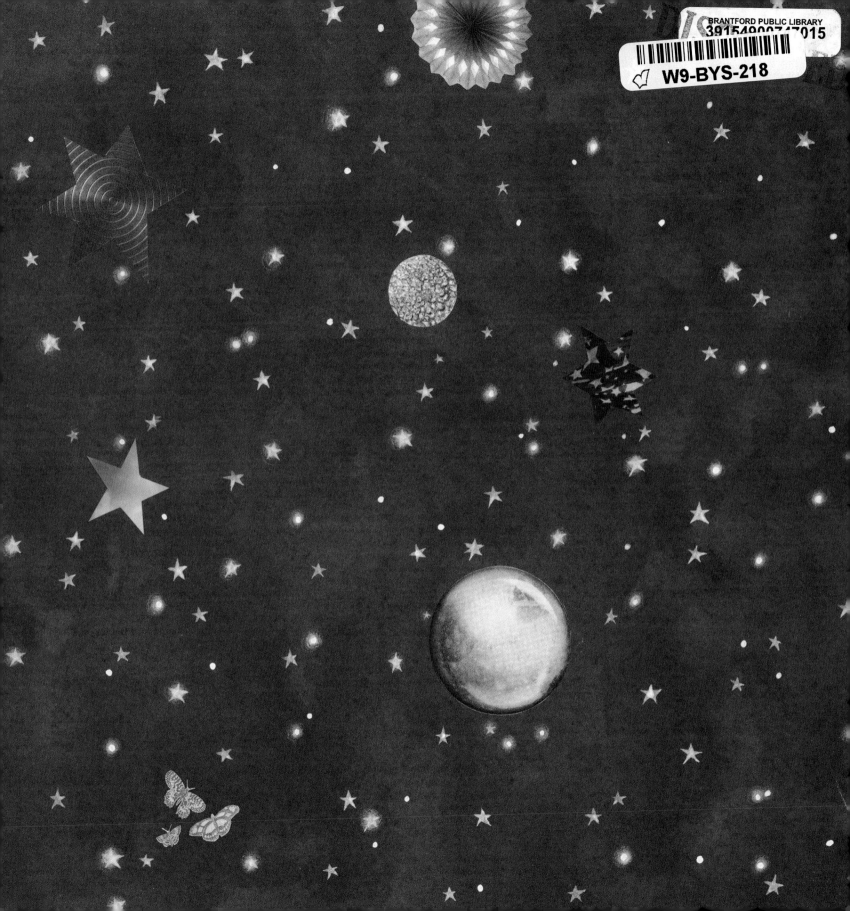

To Mom, whose strength and grace inspire me every day. ~L.J.

To Heidi and Mani, with whom I love sharing books at bedtime. ~D.M.

★

ISBN 978-1-939775-10-8

13 12 11 10   1 2 3 4 5 6 7 8 9

Printed in the United States of America

Little Pickle Stories
3701 Sacramento Street #494, San Francisco, CA 94118
Please visit us at www.littlepicklestories.com.

Design and Art Direction by Leslie L. Iorillo

Library of Congress Cataloging-in-Publication Data is available.

Yawning Yoga

Written by
Laurie Jordan

Illustrated by
Diana Mayo

Little Pickle Stories

Try to hold each pose for
three to five breaths.

Move through the poses at your own pace.

Do all the poses or choose a few
different ones to do before bedtime.

Each exercise should feel good
and get you ready for bed.

Yawning Yoga helps me unwind,
thank my body, my spirit, my mind.

So after pj's, brush, and comb,
I settle down with a gentle Om.

Connecting with the soothing sound,
Connecting with the world around.

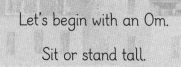

Let's begin with an Om.

Sit or stand tall.

Breathe in deeply and then exhale,
making the sound of Om
(AAAAUUUUUMMMM)
for as long as you comfortably can.

Repeat three times.

MOUNTAIN (Tadasana)

Steady and strong, a mountain so tall,
Quiet and still, I wait for nightfall.

Inhale, exhale, my breathing slows.
Rooted, reaching, air through me flows.

Stand with arms at your side and feet hip distance apart.

Keep your eyes focused on a point in front of you.

Breathe in and out, imagining you are a mountain.

HUGS & KISSES (Uttanasana)

My head drops down like the setting sun
To kiss my knees now day is done.

Fingers wrap hugs around my toes,
I take a deep breath and then my eyes close.

Start in mountain pose.

Inhale, stretching your arms up to the sky.

Exhale, folding at your hips, and let your arms dangle.

After several breaths, slowly roll back up to stand in mountain pose.

DOG-TIRED DOWN DOG
(Adho Mukha Svanasana)

It's fun to be a dog—pretend!
Down on all fours like my best friend.

I wag my tail and nod my head,
Then shake each leg and climb in bed.

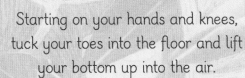

Starting on your hands and knees,
tuck your toes into the floor and lift
your bottom up into the air.

Keep your arms straight and strong.

Let your head hang loosely and
gently shake it yes and no.
Gently rock your bottom from side to side.

Lift one leg at a time and wiggle it slowly.

SEASHELL (Balasana)

Ready for rest, I curl up like a shell
My breath becomes a calming swell.

A wave rolls in, count one, two, three
A wave rolls out, back to the sea.

Start on your hands and knees, then sit
back, bringing your bottom to your heels.

Stretch your arms out in front of you
with palms down, or let your arms relax
along the sides of your body, palms up.

Rest your forehead on the floor and close your eyes.

BUTTERFLY (Baddha Konasana)

A butterfly flaps its wings in the breeze
Flexing and stretching, flying with ease.

After a ride through shining moonbeams
I settle down in time for sweet dreams.

Sit up tall and bring the soles of your feet together, forming your butterfly wings.

Breathing in—lift your knees.

Breathing out—lower your knees.

Continue "flapping" your butterfly.

BEDTIME BUG
(Ananda Balasana)

Lie on your back.

Pull your knees into your chest, and hold the outer edges of your feet with your hands.

A bedtime bug rocks to and fro.
Back and forth, with nowhere to go!

Rocking left and rocking right
helps me sleep all through the night.

Open your knees as wide
apart as your torso.

Move slowly from side to side
to massage your lower back.

JELLY BELLY (Jathara Parivartanasana)

When muscles feel all tense and tight,
I do this stretch each and every night.

I twist right round like a roll with jelly
to soothe my back, my legs, my belly.

Lie flat on your back and bring
your knees into your chest.

Open your arms out to each side,
like the letter "T".

Slowly drop your knees to the left side
and take three to five full breaths.

Slowly bring your knees back to your
chest and then drop them to the right,
taking three to five more breaths.

CANDLESTICK (Viparita Karani)

Legs be nimble, legs be quick.
Legs upright like a candlestick!

Legs be lively, legs reach high,
Flicker like flames right up to the sky.

Lie on your back and rest your legs against a wall.

Wiggle your toes.

Keep your arms down alongside your body.

To keep your neck safe, keep your eyes on your toes.

CATCH and RELEASE
(Dharana)

Like fireflies caught up in a jar,
My worries spark like little stars.

I open the lid, and worries release.
With one deep sigh, I am now at peace.

Lie on your back,
with arms at your side.

Close your eyes and relax your body.

Picture in your mind the fireflies
being released from the jar.

Let go of your thoughts or worries
so your mind is ready to rest.

Allow enough time to let
your worries fly away.

THANKFUL

(Yoga Nidra & Savasana)

To thank my body now day is done,
Each part I name, going one by one.

Relaxing down from head to toe,
Sink into the earth, and let it all go.

Lie on your back and begin by saying good night to
your face, neck, shoulders, arms, hands, and fingers.

Then say good night to your chest, ribs, and stomach.

Finally, say good night to your hips, legs, feet, and toes.

Take a big breath in and let out a big sigh "HAAAAA."
Now that your whole body feels comfortable and relaxed, close your eyes.
Be quiet and still for a few minutes.

NAMASTE

This is the way I finish the day.
Hands at my heart, I say *Namaste*.

The light in me sees the light in you.
I bow my head and my light shines through.

Bring your hands together
in front of your heart.
Say "Namaste."

AFTERWORD

The tradition of yoga began in India thousands of years ago. Loosely translated, yoga means union, or balanced connection. Yoga unifies movement of the body with the mind and spirit. More than a set of physical postures, the wider precepts of yoga can serve as a guide for a meaningful life. For hundreds of years, the benefits of yoga have spread from India to places far and wide, having a profound impact on our world. More recently, it has been discovered that yoga is particularly beneficial for children—calming the nervous system, soothing restlessness, and inviting them to be closer to themselves.

Steeped in creative and imaginative play, *Yawning Yoga* offers children simple tools to relax their bodies and focus their minds. These mindfulness techniques, breathing exercises, and yoga postures are particularly useful at bedtime, when children may need help to quiet their minds, calm their bodies, and sleep deeply. The postures found in this book will also help children learn to manage stress, soothe difficult emotions, and control impulses, When children practice yoga, they cultivate inner strength, emotional intelligence, and self-confidence. Today's overstressed, overscheduled, and overstimulated children can benefit greatly from *Yawning Yoga's* accessible and soulful approach to the practice.

—Elena Brower, Author of *Art of Attention* and *Practice You*

GLOSSARY

ADHO MUKHA SVANASANA (AH-doh MOO-kah shvah-NAHS-anna)
Adho = downward, Mukha = face, Svana = dog, Asana = pose. Downward facing dog calms the mind while stretching out the body and releasing extra energy.

ANANDA BALASANA (A-nun-da bA-lAs-anna)
Ananda = joy or bliss, Bala = child, Asana = pose. Commonly known as happy baby pose, it gently stretches the lower back and opens the hips while relieving fatigue.

BADDHA KONASANA (BAH-dah cone-AHS-anna)
Baddha = bound, Kona = angle, Asana = pose. This seated pose opens the hips while soothing the spine.

BALASANA (bah-LAHS-anna)
Bala = child, Asana = pose. Child's pose is a resting pose that stretches the hips and lower back and aids digestion.

DHARANA (da-RUH-nuh)
Dharana = concentration. Deep concentration that helps the busy mind focus on a single object, place, or idea.

JATHARA PARIVARTANASANA (ja-tha-ra pa-ri-var-ta-NAHS-anna)
Jathara = stomach, Parivarta = revolved, Asana = pose. Revolved abdomen pose soothes digestion, stretches the spine, and improves circulation.

NAMASTE (nah-muh-stey)
Nama = bow, As = I, and Te = you. Namaste means "I bow to you." Namaste is traditionally said at the end of yoga practice (with hands pressed together at the heart) to honor those we have practiced with.

OM (a-u-m)
Om is thought to be the sound of the universe. Chanting Om creates a vibration that can help shift our energy and make us feel centered and calm.

SANSKRIT (san-skrit)
The names for yoga poses come from this ancient Indian language.

SAVASANA (shvah-NAHS-anna)
Sava = corpse, Asana = pose. Corpse pose relaxes the body, mind, and spirit to reduce stress and tension.

TADASANA (tah-DAHS-anna)
Tada = mountain, Asana = pose. Mountain pose is the foundation for all of the standing postures and provides stability, confidence, and focus.

UTTANASANA (OOT-tan-AHS-anna)
Ut = intense, Tan = to stretch or extend, Asana = pose. This standing-forward bend relieves tension, calms the body and mind, and helps with insomnia.

VIPARITA KARANI (vip-par-ee-tah car-AHN-ee)
Viparita = inverted, Karani = action. Legs-up-the-wall pose uses the wall to support and soothe tired legs while calming the mind and body.

YOGA (yoh-guh)
Yoga = to yoke or bind. Yoga is often interpreted as a union and refers to the connection of breath, body, and mind.

YOGA NIDRA (yoh-guh nee-druh)
Yoga = to yoke or bind, Nidra = sleep. This practice induces full-body relaxation. It is the state between waking and sleeping.

Laurie Jordan took her first yoga class at the tender age of ten—and promptly got kicked out for laughing at the names of the poses. Who would have thought that all these years later, she would make a career out of teaching yoga? Laurie is now a social worker turned yoga teacher and children's book author. And while Laurie enjoys working with folks of all ages, she has a soft spot for kids, knowing that good habits start young. After teaching yoga to thousands of kids and training hundreds of instructors in the specialty of kids' yoga, Laurie decided to write *Yawning Yoga* to help families conquer bedtime jitters and soothe the restless child. Today, Laurie teaches yoga throughout New York and Connecticut. And she still giggles every time she says Down Dog.

Diana Mayo discovered her passion for art when she won a coloring competition at five years old. This led to much competitive drawing with her friends. Her poor dad even had to judge the competitions! She later studied graphic design and illustration at Kingston University in London, England, and has been illustrating ever since. Diana has created illustrations for magazines, design houses, greeting cards, and many children's books. She has been practicing yoga for many years and knows just how much benefit it can have for both adults and children. Yoga helps her to stretch out and relax after a long day bent over the drawing board! Diana is excited to share this book with her two children, who still need calming down at bedtime, even though they have now reached double digits.

OUR MISSION

Little Pickle Stories is dedicated to creating products that foster kindness in young people—and doing so in a manner congruent with that mission.

Little Pickle Stories
Environmental Benefits Statement

This book is printed on Appleton Reincarnation Matte Paper. It is made with 100% PCRF (Post-Consumer Recovered Fiber) and Green Power. It is FSC®-certified, acid-free, and ECF (Elemental Chlorine-Free). All of the electricity required to manufacture the paper used to print this book is matched with RECS (Renewable Energy Credits) from Green-e® certified energy sources, primarily wind.

Little Pickle Stories saved the following resources by using post-consumer, green-powered paper:

trees	energy	greenhouse gases	wastewater	solid waste
Post-consumer recovered fiber displaces wood fiber with savings translated as trees.	PCRF content displaces energy used to process equivalent virgin fiber.	Measured in CO_2 equivalents, PCRF content and Green Power reduce greenhouse gas emissions.	PCRF content eliminates wastewater needed to process equivalent virgin fiber.	PCRF content eliminates solid waste generated by producing an equivalent amount of virgin fiber through the pulp and paper manufacturing process.
54 trees	**24 mil BTUs**	**4,692 lbs**	**25,448 gal**	**1,703 lbs**

Calculations based on research by Environmental Defense Fund and other members of the Paper Task Force; applies to print quantities of 7,500 books.

 B Corporations are a new type of company that use the power of business to solve social and environmental problems. Little Pickle Stories is proud to be a Certified B Corporation.

www.littlepicklestories.com

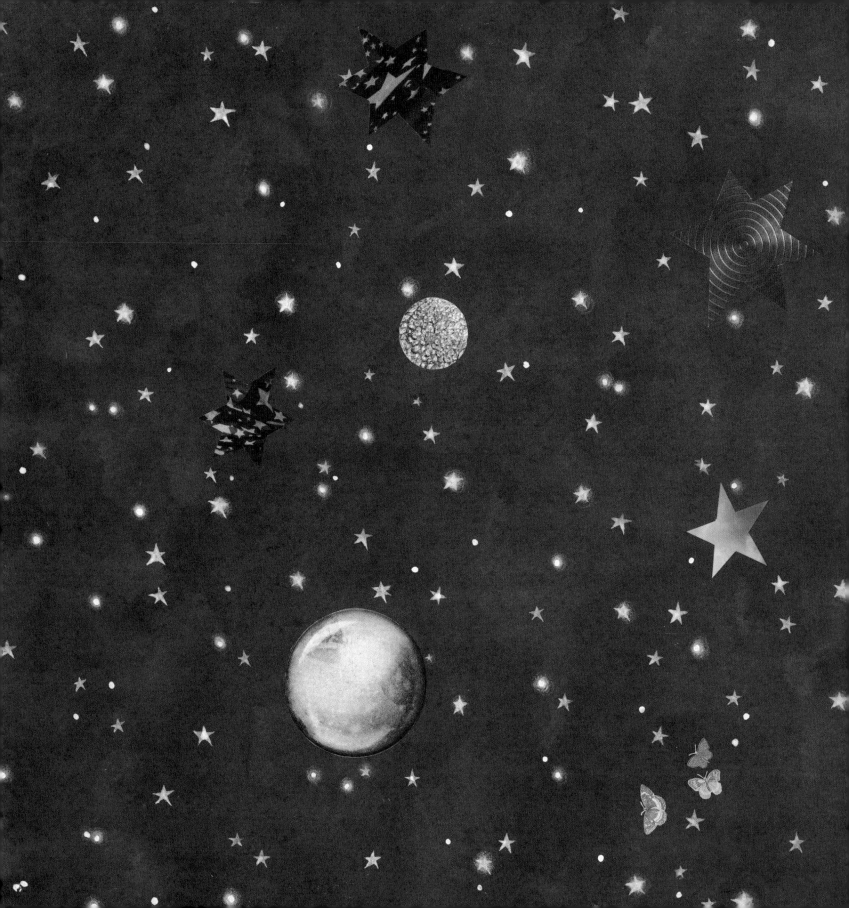